American Biographies

ELEANOR ROOSEVELT

Robin S. Doak

Heinemann
LIBRARY

Chicago, Illinois

RAP   3 2401 00871 5155

www.capstonepub.com
Visit our website to find out
more information about
Heinemann-Raintree books.

To order:
☎ Phone 888-454-2279
🖳 Visit www.capstonepub.com
  to browse our catalog and order online.

Edited by Abby Colich, Megan Cotugno, and Laura
Hensley
Designed by Cynthia Della-Rovere
Original illustrations © Capstone Global Library
  Limited 2011
Illustrated by Oxford Designers & Illustrators
Picture research by Tracy Cummins
Originated by Capstone Global Library Limited
Printed and bound in China by Leo Paper Group

16 15 14 13 12
10 9 8 7 6 5 4 3 2 1

Library of Congress Cataloging-in-Publication Data
Doak, Robin S. (Robin Santos), 1963-
  Eleanor Roosevelt / Robin S. Doak.
    p. cm.—(American biographies)
  Includes bibliographical references and index.
  ISBN 978-1-4329-6450-4 (hbk.)—ISBN 978-1-4329-
6461-0 (pbk.) 1. Roosevelt, Eleanor, 1884-1962—
Juvenile literature. 2. Presidents' spouses—United
States—Biography—Juvenile literature. 3. United
States—Politics and government—1933-1945—
Juvenile literature. I. Title.
  E807.1.R48D63 2012
  973.917092—dc23   2011037574
  [B]

Acknowledgments
The author and publishers are grateful to the
following for permission to reproduce copyright
material: Corbis: pp. 5 (© Bettmann), 9 (© Corbis),
10 (© Bettmann), 11 (© Hulton-Deutsch Collection),
14 (© Corbis), 15 (© Bettmann), 19 (© Corbis), 20
(© Bettmann), 21 (© Corbis), 23 (© Bettmann), 24
(© Bettmann), 28 (© Bettmann), 33 (© Bettmann),
38 (© Bettmann), 39 (© Bettmann), 40 (© Marvin
Koner); Franklin D. Roosevelt Presidential Library
and Museum: pp. 7, 13, 16, 17, 35; Getty Images: pp.
6 (Fotosearch), 8 (Fotosearch), 12 (Stock Montage),
26 (Rex Hardy Jr/Time Life Pictures), 30 (Time & Life
Pictures), 34 (Keystone), 36 (Leonard McCombe/
Time Life Picture); Library of Congress Prints &
Photographs Division Washington: pp. 29, 32; U.S.
Air Force photo: p. 27.

Cover photograph of Eleanor Roosevelt delivering a
radio broadcast to the American people during the
World War II reproduced with permission from Getty
Images (© Hulton-Deutsch Collection).

Every effort has been made to contact copyright
holders of material reproduced in this book. Any
omissions will be rectified in subsequent printings if
notice is given to the publisher.

Contents

Some words are shown in bold, **like this**.
These words are explained in the glossary.

Most Admired Woman

Eleanor Roosevelt first stepped into the world spotlight in 1932 as the wife of newly elected president Franklin Delano Roosevelt. But the new First Lady quickly showed that she was an important leader in her own right. She used her husband's position—and later her own fame—to champion rights for those who had no voice and to fight for peace and equality around the world. She willingly risked opposition from those Americans who felt that a First Lady should simply dress nicely and entertain at White House parties.

Eleanor spoke out for the rights of African Americans, workers, women, and other groups. During **World War II**, she became a symbol of the American woman. Today, nearly five decades after her death, Eleanor is considered one of the most important female figures of the 20th century.

Eleanor led by example, showing what people could do when they acted to make the world a better place for everyone. She once said, "I have no illusions that anyone can change the world in a short time. Yet I do believe that even a few people who want to understand, to help and to do the right thing for the great numbers of people instead of for the few can help."

Did you know?

During her lifetime, Eleanor Roosevelt was recognized in polls as the most admired woman in the world 11 times in a row.

Eleanor Roosevelt changed the role of First Lady and proved that one dedicated individual can make a big difference in the world.

Young Eleanor

Anna Eleanor Roosevelt was born on October 11, 1884, in New York City. She was the first child of wealthy parents who were from old and distinguished families. Her father, Elliott Roosevelt, was **heir** to a fortune and held no real job throughout his life. He also suffered from alcoholism. Eleanor's mother, Anna Hall, was wealthy in her own right.

Eleanor's childhood was filled with heartache. Her father and mother did not get along, and Elliott was often absent from the family. In 1892, when Eleanor was just eight, her mother died of **diphtheria**. Her little brother Elliott died just months later of the same deadly disease. Less than two years later, her father died, too. Eleanor and her baby brother, Hall, were then sent to live with their Grandmother Hall in the Hudson River Valley in New York.

After the deaths of her parents, Eleanor acted as a mother for her youngest brother, Hall, whom she called Josh.

When Eleanor was 15, she attended Allenswood, an all-girls school in London. She spent three years there.

Eleanor's grandmother was a strict guardian. She hired private tutors for Eleanor and her brother to make sure they got a good education. When Eleanor was 15, her grandmother sent her to London, England, to attend a private academy for girls.

Did you know?

Eleanor's mother was a beautiful, carefree woman who had a difficult time understanding her serious daughter, who seemed much older than her years. Anna even called her daughter "Granny," a nickname that made young Eleanor feel sad and ashamed.

Learning to help others

When Eleanor was 18, she returned to New York. She had done well at the school in London and came home a much more confident person. Teachers at the school had helped Eleanor understand the importance of courage, independence, and public service.

Eleanor joined the newly founded Junior League, an association of women who worked to improve New York City through volunteering and education. She also taught at a **settlement house** in the city. A settlement house is a community center in a poor neighborhood that provides many types of services. Eleanor also volunteered to inspect factories in the city, making sure that conditions were safe for workers.

After her return, Eleanor saw more of her distant cousin Franklin. The two had known one another since childhood. Eleanor's father had been Franklin's godfather. But now Franklin, a handsome young Harvard student, set his sights on his younger cousin. Eleanor was serious, intelligent, and shared many of Franklin's interests.

The two became engaged in 1903. Franklin's mother, Sara Delano Roosevelt, was against the marriage. But the pair would not change their minds. They married on March 17, 1905.

After returning from London, Eleanor sought ways to help those who were less fortunate than she was.

Eleanor and Franklin wed in 1905 at the home of a cousin in New York City.

Did you know?

President Theodore Roosevelt was the older brother of Eleanor's father, Elliott, who had died. At Eleanor's wedding "Uncle Ted" gave the bride away, a job usually performed by the bride's father.

A young wife

The newlyweds settled down in New York City, where Franklin soon began practicing law. In 1906 the couple welcomed their first child, a daughter named Anna Eleanor. Over the next ten years, Eleanor and Franklin would have five more children, all boys.

Franklin became involved in politics in 1910, when he was elected to New York's state senate. Eleanor helped him **campaign**. His service in the senate attracted national attention, and in 1913 he was appointed assistant secretary of the navy by President Woodrow Wilson. The family moved to Washington, D.C.

When the United States entered **World War I** in 1917, Eleanor volunteered at the American Red Cross and the Navy Relief Society in Washington, D.C. At the end of the war, she traveled to Europe with Franklin. In France she visited hospitals and toured battlefields. These experiences made her strongly hate war of any kind.

Between 1906 and 1916, Eleanor had six children. Five of the children grew to adulthood. These children were (from left to right) Elliot, Franklin, Jr., James, John, and Anna Eleanor.

After her husband's death in 1900, Sara Roosevelt relied on her son, Franklin, for companionship.

Sara Delano Roosevelt

(1854–1941)

Sara Delano Roosevelt was devoted to her only child, Franklin, born in 1882. When Franklin went away to college in Boston, Massachusetts, Sara even moved there to be closer to him. After Franklin and Eleanor's marriage, Sara controlled the couple's lives. She had a home specially built in Manhattan. One side of the home was for her to live in, while the other side was for the new couple.

Tragedy and Triumph

In 1920 Franklin was selected by the Democratic Party to run for vice president of the United States. Eleanor played a key role in the election. She worked closely with Franklin's chief adviser, Louis Howe. Together the two edited Franklin's speeches and planned his **campaign strategy**. The Democrats were defeated, however, and the Roosevelts returned to New York.

Eleanor played an important role during the 1920 presidential election, in which her husband was the candidate for vice president.

The Roosevelts were on vacation at Campobello Island in New Brunswick, Canada, when Franklin was diagnosed with polio.

Eleanor and Franklin's marriage was not always a happy one. Sara Roosevelt continued to interfere in the couple's lives. And Eleanor was upset by Franklin's close friendship with her social secretary. Although the Roosevelts stayed together, their marriage changed.

More hard times followed when Franklin was stricken with **polio** in 1921. Eleanor stayed by his side day and night, nursing him through the worst of the sickness. But the dangerous viral disease left lasting damage. Franklin would never walk again. Eleanor spent the coming months trying to boost her husband's spirits during painful physical therapy that didn't work.

Did you know?

In the early 1900s, polio was a serious health problem throughout the world. This contagious disease usually affected children. It could cause nerve damage, paralysis, and even death. In 1955 Jonas Salk invented a **vaccine** to prevent children from getting polio. A vaccine is a special type of medicine that prevents illness. As a result of the vaccine, polio is now very rare in most parts of the world.

A political helper

As her husband recovered from his illness, Eleanor kept active. To make sure that people remembered Franklin, she appeared at political events on his behalf. She attended state and national political meetings, gave speeches, and encouraged women to speak out about important issues like child labor and world peace.

In 1928 New York governor Al Smith asked Eleanor to help organize his campaign to be the next president of the United States. To replace him as governor, Smith chose Franklin. He asked Eleanor to convince her reluctant husband to run for the office. Although Smith was defeated by Republican Herbert Hoover, Franklin was elected governor of New York.

As the First Lady of New York, Eleanor still found time to do the things she loved. She taught at a school in New York City and often visited Val-Kill, her own estate in Hyde Park, New York. She also continued to help Franklin by giving speeches and making appearances around the state. When Franklin was reelected in 1930, many believed that it was Eleanor who made this possible.

Eleanor and Sara both attended Franklin's **inauguration** as New York's governor.

Eleanor shows off a chair made at Val-Kill. Her home in New York was filled with handmade furniture from Val-Kill.

Did you know?

In 1926 Eleanor and some friends started a furniture factory at Val-Kill. The company hired local farmers who were struggling to make ends meet. Val-Kill Industries produced chairs, tables, cribs, picture frames, and letter openers. Later the company added looms for weaving cloth and a **forge**. A forge is a place where metal is heated and hammered into shape.

The highest office

By 1932 the United States was in a severe **economic** crisis known as the **Great Depression**. Franklin believed that he could lead the country through this terrible period. So that year he challenged President Herbert Hoover for the top job in the nation.

Eleanor did not want her husband to become president of the United States. She told close friends that she was afraid she would lose her independence if Franklin won. Yet she publicly supported his nomination and worked to make sure that he was elected.

After Franklin won in a sweeping victory, Eleanor told the public that she was ready to move to Washington. But privately she told her friends that she did not want to be a president's wife. She did not want to give up her teaching and other work in New York.

Although Eleanor supported Franklin's desire to be president, she was secretly worried about what her role as First Lady would be.

In 1951 Eleanor stated that Louis Howe (standing on the right) helped shape her into the person she was.

Louis Howe

(1871-1936)

Reporter Louis Howe was a friend and adviser to both Eleanor and Franklin. He met the pair in 1911, when Franklin was a member of the New York Senate. Howe quickly recognized the young politician's potential and worked hard to boost his career. Howe offered the Roosevelts political and personal advice and was equally loyal to both of them. He called Franklin "the Boss" and once offered to help Eleanor become president after her husband served two terms.

The First Lady

Even before Franklin was sworn in as the 32nd president of the United States, Eleanor came under attack. Many Americans believed that a First Lady should not be publicly or professionally active. After the election, Eleanor quit her teaching job, but continued doing radio broadcasts and writing newspaper and magazine articles.

In the coming years, Eleanor would change the way people looked at the role of First Lady. She refused to merely host White House teas, dinners, and dances. Instead she reached out to Americans across the nation.

Throughout her husband's 12-year presidency, Eleanor traveled around the country and to other parts of the world. She saw firsthand the troubles of the poor, **minorities**, and laborers. She also held women-only press conferences and wrote daily and monthly newspaper columns.

Lorena Hickok

(1893–1968)

Lorena Hickok first met Eleanor during Franklin's 1932 run for the office of president. Hickok, a reporter for the Associated Press, was assigned to follow Eleanor everywhere. In time the two developed a deep respect and love for one another. At Eleanor's urging, Hickok was hired by the government to investigate how Americans were getting by during the **Great Depression**. In 1940 Hickok even moved into the White House. The two women's deep friendship lasted until Eleanor's death.

On March 4, 1933, Franklin was sworn in as president. Eleanor read and approved his famous **inaugural** speech before the event.

The New Deal

When he was running for president, Franklin had promised Americans that he would solve **unemployment**, **poverty**, and other issues. Now he put his promise into action. Immediately after taking office, he worked with Congress to put in place a series of relief and reform programs aimed at helping the nation's **economy** recover. These programs became known as the **New Deal**.

Eleanor supported the New Deal. She invited Americans to write and tell her how they were coping with the **economic** crisis. In less than a year, she received more than 300,000 letters.

Eleanor met Americans from all walks of life on her tours of the nation. Here she is visiting coal miners in Ohio.

The New Deal community of Arthurdale still exists today.

Eleanor toured the nation, checking to see how the new government programs and agencies were working. The new First Lady also visited people in poverty-stricken parts of the country. In West Virginia, she pushed the government to found a new community, Arthurdale. For Arthurdale the government gave houses, land, and farm animals to the poor people living in the region.

In her new role, Eleanor was an **advocate** for women. She **lobbied** Franklin and his advisers to appoint females to important government positions. One person she lobbied for was Frances Perkins, who was made Franklin's secretary of labor. Perkins, the first woman in U.S. history to hold such a high position, served throughout the president's terms in office.

Did you know?

Eleanor Roosevelt was the first First Lady to fly in an airplane. She even asked Amelia Earhart for flying lessons.

Equality for all

Poverty and women's rights were only two issues that Eleanor addressed. She also believed in the rights of workers and supported labor **unions**. A union is a group of workers who join together to protect their rights and interests. Eleanor's experiences as a teacher also made her an advocate for education.

Eleanor was also concerned about **civil rights**, or equal rights, for African Americans and other minorities. Throughout the nation, **segregation** was a way of life. African Americans were forced to live in different neighborhoods than whites and attend different schools. They couldn't eat at "white-only" restaurants and had to use separate bathrooms and water fountains.

Eleanor hated segregation. Everywhere she went she spoke and acted against **racism**. At one conference she moved her chair into the aisle in order to sit between the white and black sections. She quit organizations that she felt were racist. She also encouraged Franklin to seek out the advice of prominent African Americans on New Deal policies. This informal group of advisers became known as the Black Cabinet.

Fact VS. Fiction

Myth: Eleanor was a serious woman who had no sense of humor.

Fact: Eleanor enjoyed a good laugh. At many appearances, she lightened things up by telling jokes that often poked fun at herself or the president.

Eleanor resigned from a group that refused to let black opera singer Marian Anderson perform in one of its buildings.

During the second **inauguration**, Franklin and Eleanor rode in an open car in the rain to make sure that everyone who attended could see them.

An active First Lady

During her first eight years in the White House, Eleanor served as Franklin's public representative. The fact that the president couldn't walk was kept hidden from Americans, and Eleanor made many appearances that he couldn't. Her face became as famous as her husband's.

Eleanor used the opportunity to talk about the causes she loved. She was the first First Lady to take such an active, independent role in the White House. Although she was criticized by those who felt she should remain in Franklin's shadow, Eleanor reminded Americans that she was "just plain, ordinary Mrs. Roosevelt."

In 1940 Franklin decided to run for a third term. At this time, there was no law against a president serving more than two terms. However, it was a tradition since the time of George Washington that no president did so. But with **World War II** raging in Europe, Roosevelt felt that he needed to guide the country through this crisis. Eleanor reluctantly agreed with him.

Fact VS. Fiction

Myth: People believed that Eleanor's ambition for power made her push Franklin into running again and again for the presidency.

Fact: Eleanor never wanted to be First Lady of the United States. In fact, when Franklin was first elected in 1932, Eleanor told friends that she had considered divorcing him.

Eleanor and the War

In the late 1930s, people across the nation began to prepare for the possibility that the United States might enter **World War II**. Defense industries prospered as factories built weapons, ships, and other war materials. For the first time in many years, America's **economy** boomed.

Eleanor spoke to Franklin on behalf of A. Philip Randolph and other civil rights leaders to end discrimination in industry.

Eleanor flew with black pilots at the Tuskegee Institute and urged her husband to allow them to fly combat missions during the war.

While many Americans focused on concerns about the war in Europe, the First Lady spoke publicly about **discrimination** and **prejudice** in the United States. In the U.S. military, black soldiers were assigned to their own, all-black units and were not allowed to eat in the same mess halls as white soldiers. They could only hold certain positions and perform select tasks. And many business owners across the nation still discriminated against blacks.

In 1941 **civil rights** leaders told Eleanor that they were planning to march in Washington, D.C., to protest such treatment. Eleanor supported them. She spoke to Franklin about **racism** and strongly urged him to do something.

In June 1941, Franklin issued an executive order that put an end to discrimination by any company that had a contract with the government. He later formed the Fair Employment Practices Commission to ensure that companies followed his order. Some considered the commission to be a milestone (very important event) in the civil rights movement.

America's mother

The United States entered World War II on December 8, 1941, after the Japanese attack on Pearl Harbor in Hawaii. In the coming months, more than 16 million Americans took up arms in Europe and Asia. As First Lady of the land and a mother of four soldiers herself, Eleanor quickly became a symbol of hope for mothers and wives across the United States. For soldiers she became America's mother.

Franklin, Jr., and his three brothers all served in the military during World War II.

During press conferences and other appearances, the First Lady encouraged Americans to do everything they could to help the war effort. She asked them to volunteer and to buy war **bonds** to fund the U.S. military. Eleanor encouraged women to take the jobs that men left when they went off to war. And when the government began **rationing**—asking people to use only limited supplies of gasoline, food, and other items—Eleanor led the way. She made sure that the White House followed the same rationing system as the rest of the nation.

Eleanor volunteered for the Red Cross in Washington, D.C. She held fund-raisers and stood in the railroad station, handing out coffee, newspapers, and sandwiches to young men as they left for battle. The First Lady also visited wounded soldiers in hospitals in the United States and abroad.

As assistant director of the Office of Civilian Defense, Eleanor became the first First Lady to take an official government job during her husband's presidency.

Goodwill ambassador

During the war, Franklin sent Eleanor as his representative to other parts of the world. In 1942 the First Lady visited London, England, to see firsthand the damage caused by German bombing raids there. She met with King George VI and the royal family, as well as Winston Churchill and other British leaders. She toured factories and homes to see how British women were coping with the disaster.

In 1943 Eleanor made a goodwill tour of the South Pacific. On this trip, Eleanor acted as a representative of the Red Cross. The First Lady spent five weeks in the region. She made stops in Australia and New Zealand and visited 17 islands. The following year Eleanor visited military bases in the Caribbean.

In London Eleanor saw firsthand the devastation caused by warfare.

No matter where Eleanor traveled, her top priority was to visit and talk to U.S. soldiers. As the president's representative, she brought with her a message of hope and gratitude from Franklin. She toured hospitals and sat by the bedsides of wounded soldiers. Eleanor even ate dinners in the soldiers' mess halls.

Eleanor visited 17 islands on her trip through the South Pacific. On this visit, she saw about 400,000 U.S. servicemen stationed there.

Did you know?

Eleanor was unhappy with the U.S. policy of interning, or imprisoning, Japanese Americans during the war. She tried to sway the president's opinion on this issue but was not successful. She also failed to persuade the president to allow more war **refugees** from Europe into the United States.

The end of the story?

In 1944, with war still raging around the world, Franklin Roosevelt ran for a fourth term as president of the United States. He felt that he must guide the country through the war and into peace. Although Eleanor knew that her husband was suffering from serious health problems, she again supported his decision.

At this time, Eleanor was in disagreement with many of the president's advisers. Despite the war, the First Lady continued to promote **New Deal** policies and civil rights. Many of Franklin's aides felt that she was too outspoken. As a result, Eleanor did not play as much of a role in the fourth presidential **campaign** as she had in the past three.

Franklin's last **inaugural** speech was one of the shortest ever given by a president.

Eleanor watched as Franklin was sworn in on January 20, 1945. Less than three months later, she received word that the president had died while vacationing in Warm Springs, Georgia. Eleanor called Vice President Harry S. Truman to the White House, where she told him the news. Then she began making plans for Franklin's funeral and her retirement from public life. "The story is over," she told reporters.

Did you know?

After Franklin's death Congress passed the 22nd Amendment to the U.S. Constitution. This change prevented any future U.S. presidents from holding the office for more than two terms or ten total years. The new law was proposed by Congress in March 1947 and became effective in February 1951.

Eleanor, escorted by her daughter, Anna, attended Franklin's funeral in Hyde Park, New York. The president was buried in his rose garden.

First Lady of the World

After Franklin's death Eleanor expected to retire to her home in Val-Kill. She had spent most of her adult life helping her husband and working for the rights of others. Now she hoped to focus on her family, which had grown to include 13 grandchildren. However, the nation—and the world—still had a need for Eleanor Roosevelt.

In 1945 President Harry S. Truman asked Eleanor to be one of five U.S. representatives to the United Nations (UN). This newly founded organization was established to promote international cooperation and world peace. Eleanor's friends and family encouraged her to take the post.

Eleanor served in the United Nations until her resignation in 1952.

Over the next seven years, Eleanor traveled all around the globe in her new role. She saw how people lived in poor countries and nations with cruel and unfair governments. She worked hard to promote peace and human rights. President Truman called her the "First Lady of the World."

In 1948 the UN adopted the Universal **Declaration** of Human Rights, a document that Eleanor had helped write and edit. The document outlined the basic rights that all people everywhere should have. Today the declaration is still used as a guideline to measure how nations treat their citizens.

Fact VS. Fiction

Myth: Eleanor Roosevelt was not athletic.

Fact: Eleanor loved to swim, ride horses, hike, and shoot at targets. When she was younger, she played field hockey and took part in other physical activities.

Fighting hate

During the 1960s, the former First Lady continued to be committed to **civil rights**. She believed that racial **discrimination** was the biggest threat to democracy in the United States. And she fought against **prejudice** and discrimination wherever she found it.

Eleanor Roosevelt discussed many of the issues she supported on her television show.

Eleanor supported civil rights leaders and the nonviolent protests against **segregation** taking place in the South. She championed the National Association for the Advancement of Colored People (NAACP) and other groups concerned with equal rights. She met with Martin Luther King, Jr., Rosa Parks, and other activists. She made public speeches against **racism** and even visited jailed protesters.

Eleanor's support of the civil rights movement led to the Ku Klux Klan, a racist organization, placing a $25,000 bounty, or reward, on her head. Death threats against the former First Lady increased. Such threats didn't stop Eleanor, however. Racism and discrimination continued to be top issues on her mind until her death.

Did you know?

Eleanor Roosevelt's Federal Bureau of Investigation (FBI) file was one of the largest of its time. J. Edgar Hoover, the FBI's director, felt that Eleanor was a dangerous woman. The FBI investigated Mrs. Roosevelt because of her outspoken support for **unions**, African Americans, and women. The FBI also kept track of death threats against the former First Lady.

Final years

During the final years of her life, Eleanor didn't slow down. "I just don't know how," she wrote in one of her books. She traveled around the world, visiting places like Japan, India, Morocco, and Israel. She visited the Soviet Union twice, where she interviewed Soviet leader Nikita Khrushchev. The powerful leader also visited Eleanor in Hyde Park in 1959.

Eleanor gave a speech at the Democratic National Convention in 1960.

In 1960 Eleanor's doctors told her that she had **anemia** and **tuberculosis**. Despite the diagnosis, Eleanor remained active. She showed her continued support of workers' rights as well as equality for women. She also **campaigned** for presidential candidate John F. Kennedy. After Kennedy was elected, Eleanor encouraged him to appoint women to important positions in the government.

In 1961 Kennedy chose Eleanor to lead his Commission on the Status of Women. In April 1962, she made her last appearance before Congress, speaking out in favor of equal pay for women and men. Then she returned to her home, Val-Kill.

In the fall of 1962, Eleanor worked hard to finish her 27th and final book, *Tomorrow Is Now*. She died on November 7, 1962, at the age of 78. Her funeral was attended by politicians and other powerful people from around the world. She was laid to rest next to Franklin in the rose garden in Hyde Park.

Eleanor urged President John F. Kennedy to appoint more women to government offices.

A Legacy of Hope and Action

Even when overshadowed by her famous husband, Eleanor Roosevelt remained independent, active, and true to her beliefs. After her husband's death, she showed that she was still a force for change throughout the world. Her accomplishments during her lifetime improved the world and made it a better place for all human beings.

Eleanor Roosevelt's influence lives on today and continues to inspire countless people.

Eleanor's actions and words still have power today. Perhaps her most important legacy, or lasting influence, is a strong message of hope and action—even in the worst of times. In a book published in 1960, Eleanor wrote, "Surely, in the light of history, it is more intelligent to hope rather than to fear, to try rather than not to try. For one thing we know beyond all doubt: Nothing has ever been achieved by the person who says, 'It can't be done.'"

Did you know?

Eleanor Roosevelt paved the way for women to take an active role in politics and world affairs. Many important women today say they admire Mrs. Roosevelt. Among these women are Secretary of State and former First Lady Hillary Clinton, journalist Helen Thomas, and women's rights **advocate** Gloria Steinem.

Timeline

1884
Anna Eleanor Roosevelt is born on October 11.

1892
Eleanor's mother dies of diphtheria.

1894
Eleanor's father dies.

1899
Eleanor begins attending Allenswood School in England.

1902
Eleanor returns to New York, where she joins the Junior League and volunteers at a settlement house.

1903
Eleanor becomes engaged to her cousin, Franklin Delano Roosevelt.

1913
The Roosevelts move to Washington, D.C., after Franklin is appointed assistant secretary of the navy by President Woodrow Wilson.

1911
Eleanor meets Louis Howe, who will become a close friend and adviser.

1910
Franklin is elected to New York's senate.

1906
The first of Eleanor and Franklin's six children, Anna, is born.

1905
On March 17 Eleanor and Franklin marry in New York.

1916
The last Roosevelt child, John, is born.

1917
Eleanor volunteers for the Red Cross and at Washington hospitals during World War I.

1918
Eleanor offers Franklin a divorce after she learns of his relationship with another woman.

1920
Eleanor supports Franklin's failed campaign to become vice president of the United States.

1921
While vacationing in Campobello, Franklin is stricken with polio and left paralyzed.

1940
Franklin is elected to his third term as president.

1939
World War II begins in Europe.

1936
Franklin is elected to his second term as president.

1933
Eleanor begins holding all-women press conferences.

1932
Franklin is elected as the 32nd president of the United States.

1928
Franklin is elected governor of New York.

1926
Eleanor founds Val-Kill Industries at her home in Hyde Park, New York.

1941
The United States enters World War II after the bombing of Pearl Harbor.

1942
Eleanor visits London, England.

1943
Eleanor tours the South Pacific.

1944
Franklin is elected to a fourth term as president.

1945
On April 12 Franklin dies in Warm Springs, Georgia.

1945
Eleanor is appointed as one of the United Nations U.S. delegates by President Harry Truman.

1962
On November 7 Eleanor dies at a New York City hospital.

1961
President John F. Kennedy appoints Eleanor as chair of the President's Commission on the Status of Women.

1960
Eleanor is diagnosed with tuberculosis by her doctors.

1957
Eleanor visits the Soviet Union for the first time and interviews Soviet leader Nikita Khrushchev.

1948
The UN passes the Declaration of Human Rights, a document Eleanor chaired the subcommittee for drafting.

Family Tree

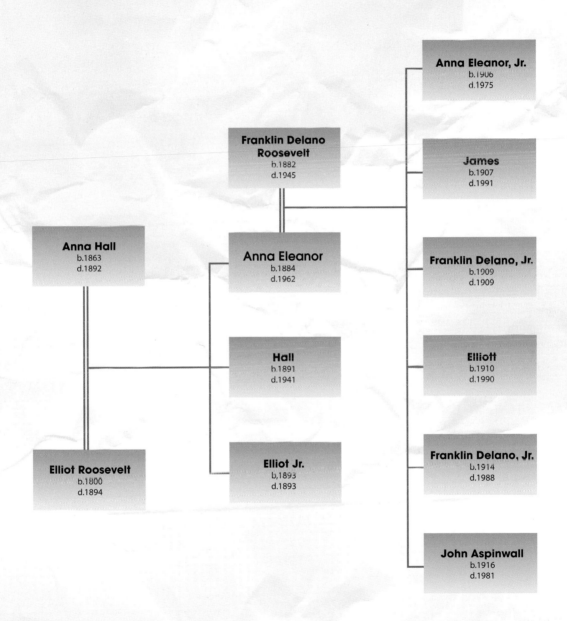

Anna Eleanor, Jr.
b.1906
d.1975

Franklin Delano Roosevelt
b.1882
d.1945

James
b.1907
d.1991

Anna Hall
b.1863
d.1892

Anna Eleanor
b.1884
d.1962

Franklin Delano, Jr.
b.1909
d.1909

Elliott
b.1910
d.1990

Hall
b.1891
d.1941

Franklin Delano, Jr.
b.1914
d.1988

Elliot Roosevelt
b.1800
d.1894

Elliot Jr.
b.1893
d.1893

John Aspinwall
b.1916
d.1981

Glossary

advocate
person who argues for a cause

anemia
medical condition affecting the blood

bond
certificate issued by the government that promises to pay back the money spent by the buyer, with interest

campaign
to try to bring about a particular result

civil rights
rights guaranteed to all U.S. citizens, regardless of race, religion, or sex

declaration
public statement

diphtheria
contagious, sometimes fatal disease caused by bacteria (germs)

discrimination
act of treating someone unfairly

economic
of or relating to production, distribution, and consumption of goods and services

economy
way an economic system is arranged

forge
place where metal is heated and hammered into shape

Great Depression
economic crisis in the United States that began in 1929 and ended in the late 1930s

heir
one who inherits property or money after the death of the owner of the property

inaugural
marking a beginning

inauguration
ceremony of inaugurating

lobby
to try to influence public officials

minority
group within a country that differs in some way (such as race, religion, or sex) from the larger part of the population

New Deal
series of policies and agencies introduced by President Franklin Roosevelt to combat the Great Depression

polio
contagious disease caused by a virus that can cause paralysis and sometimes death

poverty
state of having less money than is needed to survive

prejudice
unreasonable dislike of a group of people

racism
belief that a race of people is inferior to your own; a person who believes in racism is a racist

rationing
system of using only limited supplies of much-needed items during a time of crisis

refugee
person who has been forced to leave his or her country

segregation
policy of keeping people of different races separate from one another

settlement house
community center in a poor neighborhood that provides many types of services

strategy
planning and management of something, such as a campaign

tuberculosis
serious disease that affects the lungs and other parts of the body and that can be passed on to others

unemployment
condition of being out of work

union
group of workers who join together to protect their common rights and interests

vaccine
medicine made up of dead or weakened bacteria (germs) that is given to prevent a particular disease

World War I
war fought from 1914 to 1918 that involved all of the world's major powers

World War II
war fought from 1939 to 1945 that involved all of the world's major powers

Find Out More

Books

Connolly, Sean. *The United Nations.* Mankato, Minn.: Smart Apple Media, 2009.

Krull, Kathleen. *A Boy Named FDR: How Franklin D. Roosevelt Grew Up to Change America.* New York: Alfred A. Knopf, 2011.

Price, Sean Stewart. *Climbing Out of the Great Depression: The New Deal.* Chicago: Raintree, 2009.

Sawyer, Kem Knapp. *Eleanor Roosevelt: A Photographic Story of a Life.* New York: DK, 2006.

DVDs

The American Experience: Eleanor Roosevelt. Directed by Sue Williams. Arlington, Va.: Paramount Home Video, 2005.

Eleanor Roosevelt. Wynnewood, Penn.: Schlessinger Media, 2005.

The Eleanor Roosevelt Story. New York: Kino International Corp., 2004.

Websites

America in the 1930s
http://xroads.virginia.edu/~1930s/front.html
A website about life during the Great Depression from the American Studies department at the University of Virginia.

Arthurdale Heritage, Inc.
www.arthurdaleheritage.org
Information about Arthurdale, Eleanor's New Deal community.

Franklin D. Roosevelt Presidential Library and Museum
www.fdrlibrary.marist.edu
Home page of the presidential library, with information on Eleanor.

The Eleanor Roosevelt Papers Project
www.gwu.edu/~erpapers/
Information about the life and career of Eleanor Roosevelt from George Washington University.

National First Ladies Library
www.firstladies.org
Information about Eleanor Roosevelt, Michelle Obama, and other First Ladies.

Internet Archive
www.archive.org/search.php?query=Eleanor%20Roosevelt%20 AND%20collection%3Anewsandpublicaffairs
A place to view video clips of former First Lady Eleanor Roosevelt.

Places to visit

The Franklin D. Roosevelt Presidential Library and Museum
4079 Albany Post Road
Hyde Park, NY 12538
845-486-7770
www.fdrlibrary.marist.edu

Eleanor Roosevelt National Historic Site
4097 Albany Post Road
Hyde Park, NY 12538
800-337-8474
www.nps.gov/elro/index.htm

United Nations Headquarters
Visitors Center
1st Avenue at 46th Street
New York, NY 10017
212-963-8687
www.un.org/en/

Smithsonian Institution's First Ladies Exhibit
National Museum of American History
National Mall, 14th Street and Constitution Avenue NW
Washington, DC 20013
202-633-1000
http://americanhistory.si.edu/exhibitions/exhibition.cfm?key=38&exkey=1239

Index